Cup Cooking

Individual Child-Portion Picture Recipes

Barbara Johnson, *author*
Betty Plemons, *illustrator*

TX
652
.5
J6

Acknowledgments

We give our sincere thanks to the many people who helped with this book, especially the following:

Mrs. Betty Fisher for the gift of her typing.

Mr. W.E. Crowson, "senior printer" at Fletcher Printing, for helpful suggestions and guidance.

Flagship Bank of Lake Alfred for copying test recipes.

Juanita Geathers for developing recipes, namely: Peanut Honey Balls, Toasted Shapes, Drazzle Sandwich, Instant Pudding, Cheese 'n Blanket, Jello, Fruit Salad, Cheese Toast.

Betty Plemons for the monumental task of preparing the graphics.

Bev Veitch for permission to use the recipe, "Honey Wheat Bread", from *A Child's Cook Book,* 656 Terra California Drive #3, Walnut Creek, California 94595.

We thank the teachers, special educators, nutritionists, school administrators, lay persons, friends, acquaintances and the Polk Association on Children Under Six for the acceptance of *Cup Cooking* and the encouragement which prompts this printing.

We are indebted to nutritionists at the INSTITUTE OF FOOD AND AGRICULTURAL SCIENCES at the UNIVERSITY of FLORIDA for preparing the information on recipes relative to U.S.D.A. Food Pattern Guidelines.

Barbara Johnson

TABLE OF CONTENTS

PREFACE

"Cooking is the foundation activity for language growth among children who need language activities. More than any other pursuit available to teachers, cooking assures a language base that includes all the class. It is the only activity parents and teachers can pursue on a regular basis that uses all the descriptive characteristics of language...the activity that has the greatest carryover into reading. They're all there; nouns, verbs, adjectives, adverbs, etc., used to describe the what, how, where and why, the movements, textures, tastes and feelings that go into preparing something good to eat."

Dr. Roach Van Allen
Language Development and Reading Specialist
University of Arizona at Tucson

Food preparation and tasting experiences are central to developing a child's awareness of a variety of foods. Early experiences with foods establish attitudes and behavior patterns which have lasting influence. A program for children which includes cooking is fun, informative and valuable for them.

Jean Crum Jones, M.P.H., R.D.
Consulting Nutritionist
Valley Nutrition Consultants
Derby, Connecticut

5

Introduction

Why These Recipes?

These individual portion recipes have been *developed for and tested by young children in day care centers, pre-schools, kindergartens and elementary schools.*

Our aim has been to provide recipes for foods that:

1. Are wholesome and nutritious - energy producing, body building, and regulating.
2. Include the Four Basic Food Groups:
   - Fruits and vegetables
   - Breads and cereals
   - Milk and milk products
   - Proteins - meat, fish, eggs, dry peas, beans, nuts.
3. Suitable for mid-morning snacks.
4. Simple to prepare.
5. Economical

Why Individual-Portion Recipes?

1. Each child can measure, mix, manipulate and consume one complete portion.

2. Following sequenced picture steps the child can move through the activity with a minimum of adult guidance.

3. The child is having a rewarding beginning reading experience as he is challenged to "read" the directions, utensils and materials at each station.

4. The beginning reader or non-reader can "keep the place" with sequenced steps. His whole body moves left to right from one station to the next.

5. The method allows for pupil independence in achievement of success.

6. It provides for teaching based on the ideas that:
   - Children learn best when given one concept at a time.
   - Children need to manipulate things themselves.
   - Children learn best in a one-to-one situation.
   - Children need to learn through their own language and thought processes.

First, wash hands   **Level measures**

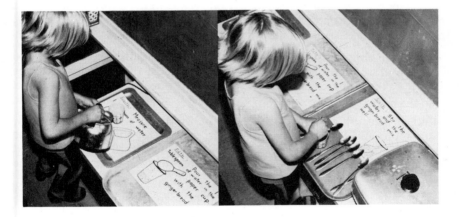

Following sequenced picture steps, child can work with minimal adult guidance.

Photos by Merseal

How Do You Start?

1. *Select a recipe* with few steps. *Lemonade, Dried milk,* or *Gingerbread* are good starters.

2. *Prepare Charts:*
On 5'' by 8'' cards or half sheets of typing paper prepare a separate chart for each step of the recipe. Where three tablespoons of an ingredient are called for trace the outline of three tablespoons on the chart.

For teacher's convenience include on each chart the recipe name, sequence ordinal number and teacher's name. See Appendix for full size sample chart.

3. *Laminate* on both sides at the school media center or with clear contact paper. Laminate one-half inch beyond the edge, fully sealing the paper against moisture. (Spills can be sponged off as children clean up.)

4. *Collect the supplies* to be used at each station in the recipe sequence. Paper cups or margarine tubs are good mixing bowls. The cups used for mixing and baking are the 5 oz. paper cups commonly used in bathroom cup dispensers. The small amount of wax that melts from these cups is negligible and can easily be cleaned from the skillet after baking. Smaller 3 oz. cups are used for mixing dips as they are less expensive. Small margarine bowls are good for stiff mixtures like peanut butter and bread dough.

4. *Lay out the sequenced steps* from left to right. At each station set out the equipment and supplies to complete that step. Where necessary, place ingredients in small containers easy for children to handle.

Place appropriate measuring spoon on each outline. If a child is to measure more than one spoonful at a station, the filled leveled spoon is placed back on the chart outline until all are filled. Then the item is put into the mixing container.

When measuring liquids, the spoons to be used are placed in a bowl. As a spoonful is measured and emptied, the used spoon is placed on the spoon outline on the chart. As a child measures each of the required number of spoonsful, he is building or strengthening his concept of the number.

6. *Name Label.* Print child's name with permanent felt market on:
   • Paper label, and staple to paper cup to be used in baking.
   • foil wrapped cardboard baking sheets.
   • masking tape labels on bowls to be refrigerated.
   • on toothpick and paper flags for oven baked items.

What Do You Need To Know Before You Start?

Individual portion baked goods can be *mixed and baked* in a five ounce paper cup. They bake satisfactorily in a covered electric skillet. The rim on the bottom of the cup prevents the item burning on the bottom. Set the temperature high as the skillet lid is continually being removed to add each child's completed recipe. A portable oven may be used, but it is easier to add and remove a sequence of small items from the skillet than from the oven. ONLY THE TEACHER HANDLES THE HEATED APPLIANCES.

The first time a recipe is used, the teacher, or one child, works through the sequence as a demonstration for the four to six children who will be the first to use the recipe. This demonstration is repeated with each group entering the center. Directions are interpreted, techniques demonstrated. Children learn to level dry ingredients by scraping (not packing) with a tongue depressor, etc.

Each time a group uses a recipe less adult supervision is needed. Adult observation is recommended. The timely question or comment from the teacher adds meaning to the experience and is sometimes necessary to help solve a problem.

Once children have learned to move from left to right and follow chart directions, an activity can be used to emphasize a variety of learnings. Each subsequent time a recipe is used a specific learning may be stressed.

Potential of Cup Cooking

Science Skills:
- Observing, classifying, measuring, inferring, predicting, communicating to transfer information.
- At each step check color, feel, taste, smell.
- Note changes: How did cooking change the apple?
        What happened to the sugar when stirred
        in the water?
- Note similarities and differences.
- Note physical properties of matter.
    Dry ingredients need to be leveled. Do liquids need to be leveled? Why not? (Liquids level themselves.) Do not tell the children, allow them to discover for themselves. Simple questions can stimulate their thinking and verbalization of discoveries.

9

Math Skills

- One to one correspondence.
- More or less.
- Bigger or smaller.
- The concept of number—3 spoons full, 5 raisins.
- Measuring.
- Estimating
- Fractions.

Reading and Pre-Reading Skills

- **Language Development**

  Encourage children's comments on the appearance, smell, feel, taste at each stage of a recipe to help them develop descriptive language. Help them develop the language that tells the what, how, when, where and why of the movements, textures, tastes of the foods experience.

- **Directional Prepositions**

  Above, below, in, beside, under, in front of,...
  When measuring dry ingredients ask, "Is the...piled *above* the edge of the spoon?" "It needs to be level with the edge of the spoon." Demonstrate leveling with the straight edge. Also demonstrate attempted leveling as children do by scooping from the spoon. Ask, "Is this level with the edge of the spoon? No, the...is *below* the edge of the spoon."

  "When leveling where should we hold the measuring spoon, *beside* the bowl or *above* the bowl?"

  "When adding the...to the mixing cup do we hold the spoon *above* the cup (the children tend to, thus spilling) or put it *in* the cup before tipping the...out?,,

  Measuring liquids in measuring cups, ask, "Is the liquid at the line, *above* the line or *below* the line?"

- **Sequencing Skills**

  Practice the language of sequence when introducing the recipe to the small group.

  "This is the *first* chart. Look at the things on the *first* tray. What do you do here at the *first* step?"..."What do you do *after* ...?" "What is the *next* thing to do?"

  "This is the *next* step, the *second* step." etc. Later in the day study and analyze the shuffled recipe charts to recall the sequence followed.

  "Find the chart that shows what to do *first.*"

  "Find the chart that shows what to do *next.*"

  "Find the chart that shows what to do *after* you measure the water..."

  "What was the *last* chart?"

10

- **Distinguish Between Letter, Word Sentence**

    After a cooking experience study the charts for their letter word and sentence content. The charts have meaning for the children after the cooking experience.
    - Looking at a single chart have children identify letters they know. "Put together this way those letters say..."
    - Teacher can read all words, phrases, sentences for the children.
    - Prepare word and phrase cards using words and phrases for a recipe in current use. In small groups lay out recipe charts. Let group members draw a word or phrase card to match to the coinciding recipe chart.
    - Give children an opportunity to shuffle all word cards and attempt to read same. Any child who can read a card may have that word or phrase for his/her personal word card box.
- **Food Preparation and Nutrition Skills —
Jean C. Jones, M.P.H., R.D.**
    - Cooking can be and should be fun. Children need to explore food for stimulation and for discovering something new and interesting. Creating something good to eat is a rewarding experience for a child.
    - In today's society, commercial advertising glamorizes poor eating habits and relatively non-nutritious foods. Children need to learn to choose and prepare foods which build good health. These habits are not acquired naturally; they must be learned.
    - Eating a variety of healthful foods is the way to achieve good nutrition. The four food groups provide a guide for selecting the foods we need for growth and good health.
    - Cooking in school and at home enhances school-home ties. Children gain skills and perceptions that can be practiced and developed in both settings.
- **Addendum 1990**
    - Bend spoons for liquids: Keep certain spoon handles bent up ladle-fashion for liquid measuring — much easier for children to measure that way.
    - Flour Shaker: For flouring hands or work surface use a flour shaker.
    - Older School Age Children: Double some of these recipes or let children make 2 servings to meet appetites of older school age children.

The teaching-learning possibilities of the **Cup Cooking** technique are limited only by time and imagination. However do not kill the project with discussion. Remember, children learn best when given one concept at a time.

Cup Cooking Workshop Consultant Available, Contact
Early Educators Press • P.O. Box 1177 • Lake Alfred, Florida 33850
Phone: (813) 956-1569

Gingerbread

(If egg called for omit in this recipe.)

A. 3 T. Gingerbread Mix

put mix in paper cup

B. 1 T. Water

add to cup

C. stir well

D. Bake: 400,° 15 minutes or until done

Pineapple Upsidedown Gingerbread

A. 1 t. Salad Oil

pour in paper cup

B. 1 t. Brown Sugar

sprinkle on oil

C. 1 T. Crushed Drained Pineapple

Spread on top of sugar

D. In seperate bowl or cup, prepare Gingerbread (above) thru step three. Add, but do not mix. Bake (same)

12

Pancakes

A. 2 T. Pancake Mix

put in bowl

B. 2 T. water

add...

C. Mix together until fairly smooth do not over mix

D. note: For one small pancake, 1 T. mix, 1 T. water is adequate. Mix in 3oz paper cup to avoid dishwashing

E. grease hot skillet pour pancake batter

F. turn when edges are cooked and bubbles on top. for variations see package

Baking Powder Biscuits

A. 1/3 cup Flour — put in bowl

B. 1/2 t. Baking Powder — add..

C. 2 T. Powdered Milk — add..

D. 1 pinch Salt — add

E. Mix

F. 1 T. Oil — pour in cup not in bowl!

G. 2 T. Water — add to oil in cup

H. pour liquids into dry mix. stir

I. flour hands Knead dough on lightly floured table roll or pat into 3 ○○○ Biscuits

J. place on oiled pan Name bake: 10-15 min. 450°

Baking Powder Biscuit Variations

A. Cheese Biscuits

1 T. Grated Cheese

add to dry ingredients

B. Orange Biscuits

1/3 t. Grated Orange Rind

add to dry ingredients.

Butterscotch Pinwheels

A.

pat or roll dough 1/4" thick.

B. 1 t. soft Margarine

spread on dough

C. 1 T. Brown Sugar

put in cup

D. 1/4 t. Cinnamon

add to cup   Mix

E. sprinkle sugar and cinnamon on dough.

roll___. cut into 3 slices

F. place cut side down in greased muffin tins or paper muffin cups.

bake in 425° oven 15 min. Remove - invert.

Ginger Cookies

A. 1 T. Sugar

B. 1 T. Margarine — mix well

C. 1 T. Molasses — stir

D. 1 t. Beaten Egg — mix well

E. 1 T. Milk — stir

F. 1/4 t. Vinegar

G. note: vinegar curdles milk — stir well

H. 1/2 cup Flour — pour flour into sifter which has been set in pan. Do not sift now

I. 1/4 t. Ginger — Do Not sift

J. 1/4 t. Baking Soda — Do Not sift

K. Sift flour, soda, ginger into mixture in bowl

Continued on next page

Ginger Cookies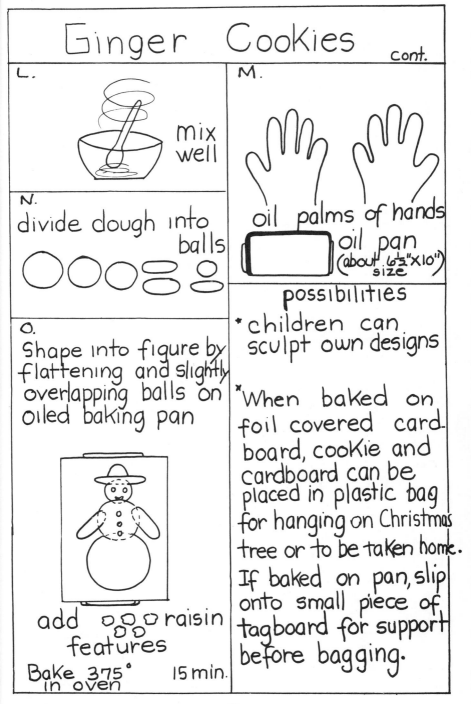

cont.

L.

mix
well

M.

oil palms of hands

oil pan
(about 6½"x10"
size)

N.

divide dough into
balls

O.

Shape into figure by
flattening and slightly
overlapping balls on
oiled baking pan

add ⬭⬭⬭ raisin
features

Bake 375°   15 min.
in oven

possibilities

* children can
  sculpt own designs

* When baked on
  foil covered card-
  board, cookie and
  cardboard can be
  placed in plastic bag
  for hanging on Christmas
  tree or to be taken home.

If baked on pan, slip
onto small piece of
tagboard for support
before bagging.

17

Milk and Honey Bread

A. 1 t. Yeast
put in bowl

B. 2 t. Honey
add

C. 2 T. Warm Water (105°)
stir until dissolved

D. 2 T. Oil
add

E. 2 T. Evaporated Milk
add

F. 1 pinch Salt
add

G. 1 pinch Ginger
add

H. 1/3 cup Flour
add

Continued on next page

Milk and Honey Bread Cont.

I.

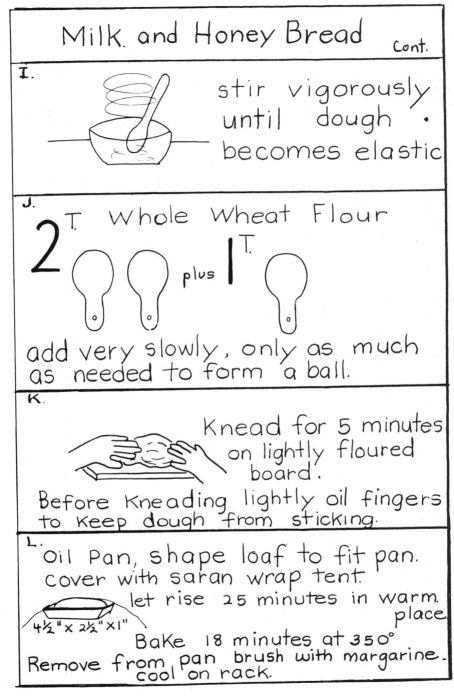

stir vigorously until dough . becomes elastic

J.

2 T. Whole Wheat Flour

plus 1 T.

add very slowly, only as much as needed to form a ball.

K.

Knead for 5 minutes on lightly floured board.

Before Kneading lightly oil fingers to keep dough from sticking.

L.

Oil Pan, shape loaf to fit pan. cover with saran wrap tent.

4½" x 2½" x 1"

let rise 25 minutes in warm. place.

Bake 18 minutes at 350°

Remove from pan brush with margarine. cool on rack.

Molasses Muffins

A. 1 T. Flour
put in cup

B. 1 1/4 of 1/4 t. Baking Soda
add 1/4

C. 1 pinch Salt
add

D. Mix well

E. 2 T. Bran
add bran..mix

F. 1 T. Milk
add..

G. 1 t. Molasses plus 1/2 t.

H. 10 Raisins
add

I. stir

J. bake in paper cup in covered skillet 30-40min. 375°

20

Lemonade

A. 1/4 cup Water

pour into <u>clear</u> plastic glass

B 1 t. sugar or honey

add to water

C. stir until dissolved

pour solution into paper cup

D. 2 t. Lemon Juice

add juice to cup

E. 1 Ice Cube

add.

F. M-M GOOD!

stir - enjoy!

Stuffed Celery

A.

Celery

*cut celery

3 inches

< 8 centimeters

*children might enjoy measuring

B.

Stuff with one of these

PEANUT BUTTER

CREAMY COTTAGE CHEESE

Super Sardine Spread
* see recipe

Mashed Avocado

Pineapple cheese Spread
*see recipe

"Walking" Salads

A. Prunes

stuffed with peanut butter

B. Cheese Stix or Spam

wrapped in lettuce leafs

Kabobs
fruits and toothpicks

(arms and legs added for fun only)

melon Balls

prune, melon pineapple wedge

pineapple wedge melon Balls

Vegetable Sandwiches

Cucumber spread with Cream Cheese

carrot curls spread with peanut butter

Celery stuffed with cheese

Note: the variety is endless. All kinds of raw fruits and vegetables can be used with many kinds of fillings. let children make their own combinations.

Apple Salad

A.

$\frac{1}{4}$ Apple

cut apple into small pieces

B.

Small piece Celery

chop celery into small pieces

C.

5 add Raisins

D.

1 t. Mayonnaise

add..

E.

Mix Well

EAT!

caution: cut down on cutting board.

to vary:
substitute or add.

* ½ t. chopped nuts
* 1 T. Shredded Cabbage
* 1 T. Crushed Pineapple
* 1 T. Grated Carrot

24

first

wash

Gingerbread

Wash Hands

Supplies and Equipment

- Wash basin or sink or water filled spray bottle.
- Soap
- towels
- trash can

Suggested Learnings

- First step in sequence
- Always wash hands before handling food.
- Wash well with soap and water to prevent spread of germs, colds and other illness

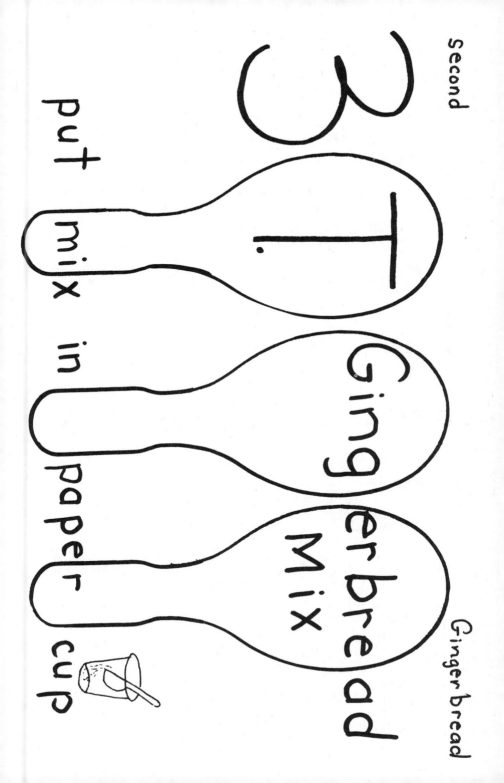

3

T.

Gingerbread
Mix

put mix in paper cup

Gingerbread

3 T. Gingerbread

Supplies and Equipment

- Bowl of gingerbread mix
- 3 measuring tablespoons
- tongue depressor (for leveling)
- name-labeled 5 oz. paper cups for each child
- All above items on one tray with chart.

Suggested Learnings

- three: numeral amount
- meaning of level
- dry ingredients
- measuring
- tablespoon
- Observe
  - color   feel
  - taste   smell

third

Gingerbread

add to cup

water

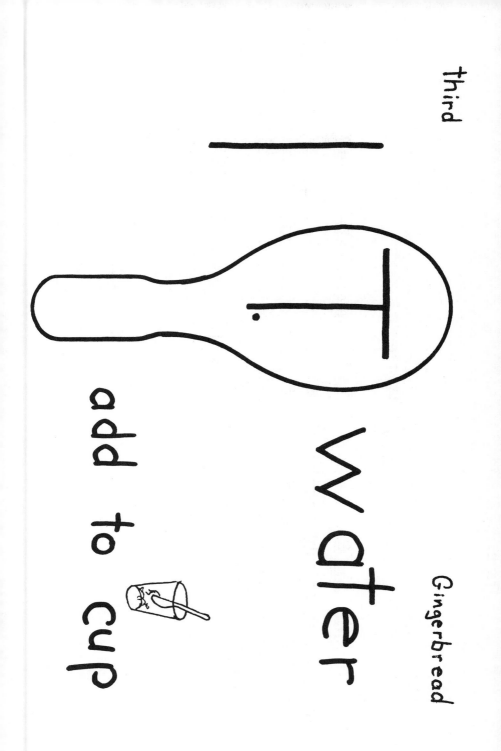

1 T. Water

Supplies and Equipment

- 1 measuring tablespoon
- small pitcher of water
- All above items on tray with chart.

Suggested Learnings

- liquid
- pouring practice- use spout
- Observe:
  - Liquid levels itself.
  - Does water mix with flour readily?
    Must it be stirred to mix completely?

fourth

Stir

well

or

Bake: 400° 15 min.

'till done.

Gingerbread.

Stir Well, Bake

Supplies and Equipment

- Tray with chart and teaspoons for stirring.
- Electric skillet

As soon as gingerbread is well mixed teacher places cup in pre-heated dry electric skillet. Cover. Teacher check for doneness- When done springs back from touch.

Suggested Learnings

- Stir; mix
- Observe:

change in - color
    feel
    taste
    smell

As lid is removed during baking, note change in size (rising in cup)

Cole Slaw

A. Cabbage Carrots

shred amount needed
Children operate shredder

B. 1 T. slaw Mix

put slaw into paper cup

C. 1 Salt pinch

add salt to cup

D. 1/2 t. Mayonnaise

add to slaw mix

E. Stir

EAT!

F. Raisins 6

add one

Variations

Apple (diced) 1 T.

Bell Pepper (diced fine) 1 t.

Pineapple (crushed) 1 t.

or more of these to slaw.

Fruit Salad

A. 1/3 Banana

put banana slices in bowl

B. 1/4 Apple

chop apple

add to bowl

C. 1/4 Peach (or Nectarine)

add chopped peach to bowl

D. 1 Orange Section (and or Grapefruit)

add chopped orange to bowl

E. stir

EAT!

notes:
Be sure children wash hands and fruit.
Peel if necessary.
Cut in small pieces.

One half the class can bring in enough fruit to serve everyone or: each child can bring one piece for Friendship salad at Thanksgiving

26

Potato Salad

A. boiled potato

1/4 cup

put cold diced potato in paper cup

B. Seasonings

2 pinches each:

salt · Celery Seed · Parsley

add seasonings to cup

C. Prepared Mustard

1 t. 1/4

add to cup

D. Grated Onion

1 t. 1/4

add to cup

E. Vinegar

1 t. 1/4

add to cup

F. Mayonnaise

1 T.

add to cup

G. refrigerate

Mix   2 hours

To Vary: add

2 t. chopped celery or Bell Pepper

Baked Apple

A. 1/2 Apple
cut crossways

B. core apple

C. place apple, cut side down in oiled skillet.

D. 5 Raisins
put in hole of apple

E. 1 t. Sugar
pour in hole

F. 1 Cinnamon pinch
sprinkle on sugar

G. 1 T. Water
pour water to side of apples

H. cover skillet bake until soft.. at 350°

Apple Sauce

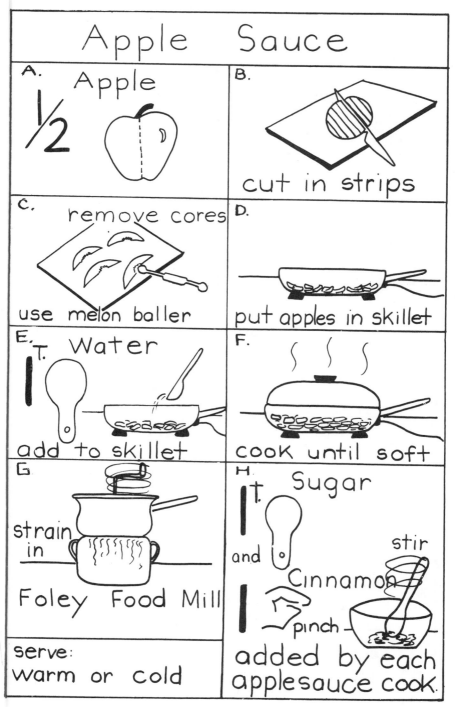

A. 1/2 Apple

B. cut in strips

C. remove cores — use melon baller

D. put apples in skillet

E. 1 T. Water — add to skillet

F. cook until soft

G. strain in Foley Food Mill

H. 1 T. Sugar and 1 pinch Cinnamon — stir — added by each applesauce cook.

serve: warm or cold

Friendship (Stone) Soup

one half class bring in one vegetable. Wash and peel only if necessary. Peeling wastes vitamins

A. $\frac{1}{2}$ Potato
cut into small pieces (or)

$\frac{1}{2}$ Carrot
chop in pieces (or)

Vegetables (any you choose)

B. add to friends vegetables in large pot or electric skillet

C. $2^{T.}$ Water
each child adds 2 T water to soup

D. 2 Bouillon Cubes
teacher adds these

E. cover cook slowly till tender

enjoy

Stone Soup: start with scrubbed smooth stone.

Chocolate Milk

A. Powdered Milk

3 T.

pour powdered milk into 5 oz paper cup

B. Instant Chocolate Mix

1 t. plus 1/2 t.

Instant Chocolate Mix

add chocolate mix to cup

C. Water   Ice Cube

1/3 cup   plus 1

add water and ice cube to cup

D. __Cocoa__

stir   well   replace cold water with warm water.

31

Butter

A. 1 T. Whipping Cream

pour cream into baby food jar

B. cover tightly. shake until butter forms

C. pour off liquid into bowl

D. serve plain on cracker or bread

or add 1 pinch salt

then serve

note: Teacher might want to put larger amount in pint jar and let children take turns shaking.

Pineapple Cheese Spread

A. 1 T. Crushed Pineapple

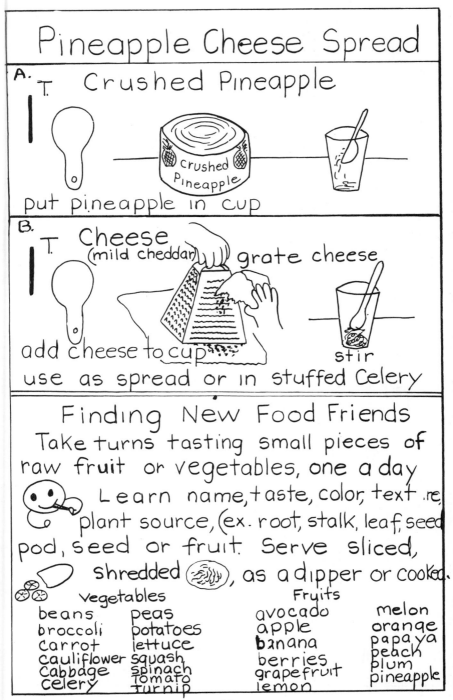

put pineapple in cup

B. 1 T. Cheese (mild cheddar) grate cheese

add cheese to cup   stir

use as spread or in stuffed celery

Finding New Food Friends

Take turns tasting small pieces of raw fruit or vegetables, one a day. Learn name, taste, color, texture, plant source, (ex. root, stalk, leaf, seed pod, seed or fruit. Serve sliced, shredded, as a dipper or cooked.

Vegetables		Fruits	
beans	peas	avocado	melon
broccoli	potatoes	apple	orange
carrot	lettuce	banana	papaya
cauliflower	squash	berries	peach
cabbage	spinach	grapefruit	plum
celery	tomato	lemon	pineapple
	turnip		

33

Cottage Cheese Dip

A. 1 T. Cottage Cheese

put in cup

B. 1/2 t. Milk (may omit)

add to cup

C. 1/4 t. Lemon or Lime Juice

add to cup

D. 1 pinch Celery Salt

add to cup

E. 1 pinch Dried Sage

add to cup

F. 1 pinch Onion Flakes or Grated onion

add

G. Mix

H. Dip up on fruit or vegetable chunks or spread on crackers.

Instant Pudding

A. 2 T. Instant Pudding Mix

B. 2 T. Dry Milk — stir

C. 1/3 cup water — pour in cup

D. stir 2 minutes — cool in refrigerator

Jello

A. 1 T. + 1 t. Jello

B. 1/4 cup hot water — pour in cup

C. stir until dissolved

D. 1 ice cube — add to cup stir until melted

five Refrigerate until set.

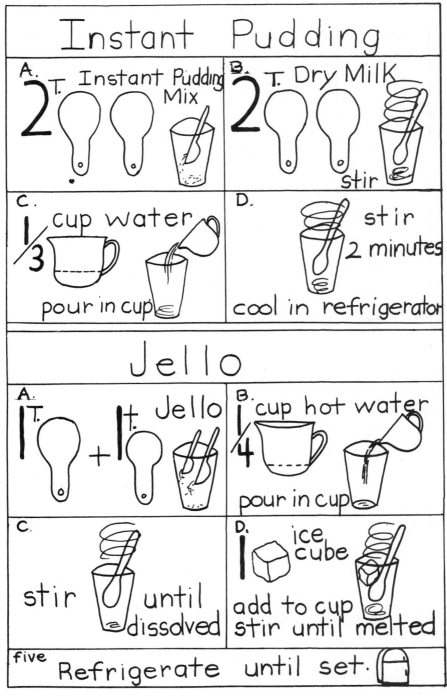

35

Peanut Butter

A. Peanuts

10

B. Shell Peanuts

two per shell

you can count!

C. grind peanuts

D. Peanut Oil

1 t.

add to ground peanuts

E. Salt

1

F. Mix

G. spread on crackers or bread or use as dip.

Peanut Honey Balls

A. 1 T. Peanut Butter

put in bowl

B. ½ t. Honey

add honey

C. Powdered Milk
1 t. + ½ t.

add milk

D. mix well

E. Roll

into balls

F. 5 Wheat Cheks

crush wheat chex with rolling pin

roll balls in crushed wheat chex

Scrambled Egg

A. Egg — crack egg over bowl

B. 1 T. Milk — add to egg

C. 1 pinch Salt — add

D. stir

E. pour into oiled "Pam" treated skillet.. Low heat

Four or five children combine egg mixtures in skillet. Take turns stirring with wooden spoon.

Variations

* serve on buttered toast.

when partly cooked, add one of the following

* grated cheese   * snipped parsley   * diced ham

Egg Salad

To Cook eggs:
* have eggs at room temperature.
* place eggs in pan. add cool water to
* cover pan, bring water rapidly to boil. cover.

* turn heat to <u>very low</u>, let stand
   covered 20 minutes (High heat toughens egg)
* cool immediately in cold water.

A. Egg
Crack and
peel egg

B. dice egg
put in cup

C. 1 T. diced
Celery
or
Bell
Pepper
add to cup

D. pinch
salt
add...

E. 2 t. Mayonnaise
add...

F. EAT!
Mix

Super Sardine Spread

one

1 T. drained water-packed Mashed **Sardines**

put in paper cup

B.

1/2 t. Lemon Juice

add to cup

C.

1 t. Chopped Pickle

add to cup

D.

1 t. Mayonnaise

add to cup

E.

mix

F.

spread on 3 crackers

or stuff celery

or roll in lettuce leaf

Tuna Salad

A. Chunk Tuna

2 T.

put tuna in bowl

B. Chopped Celery

1 T.

add to tuna

C. Mayonnaise

1 T.

add to tuna

D. Pickle Relish

1 t.

add...

E. Lemon Juice

1/4 T. + 1 pinch onion flakes + 1 pinch salt

add...

F.

Mix

M-M-good

Eat on crackers

To Vary: Egg and Tuna Salad:
   add ½ hard cooked egg
   1 pinch parsley flakes
*Substitute drained canned Mackeral
for Tuna... economical and nutritious

Toasted Shapes

A. Honey Graham

place on baking sheet

B. Slice Cheese

place cheese on cutting board

C. cut cheese with cookie cutter

D. place cheese shape on Honey Graham

E. place pan in oven bake until... 350°

F. Cheese Melts

M-M-good

Cheese Toast

A. 1/2 Slice Bread

B. 1/2 Slice Cheese

C. place on baking sheet

D. Broiler Oven

Teacher put pan in oven. broil until cheese melts

Drazzle Sandwich

A. 1/2 Slice Bread
place on baking dish

B. 1/2 Slice Cold Meat
place meat on bread

C. 1/2 Slice Cheese
place cheese on meat

D. Bake in 350° oven
until cheese melts

Cheese n/Blanket

A. 1 Slice Dried Beef
place on waxed paper

B. 1 Cheese Stick
cheese
roll cheese in dried beef

C. place toothpick into roll

D. bake in 350° oven 5 minutes
oven

Cheesey Weiner Wheels

A. spread small amount tomato paste on cracker

B. Cheese — cut slice of cheese into 1/4's with knife.

C. place cheese on cracker

D. Weiner — cut weiner with knife

E. place weiner slice on cheese

F. place in 350° oven... bake until cheese melts.

Variations
* Try various kinds of cheese.
* bologna.. etc, in place of weiner
* A variety of crackers
* substitute salad dressing for tomato paste.
* Try putting cheese on top.

44

Personal Pizza

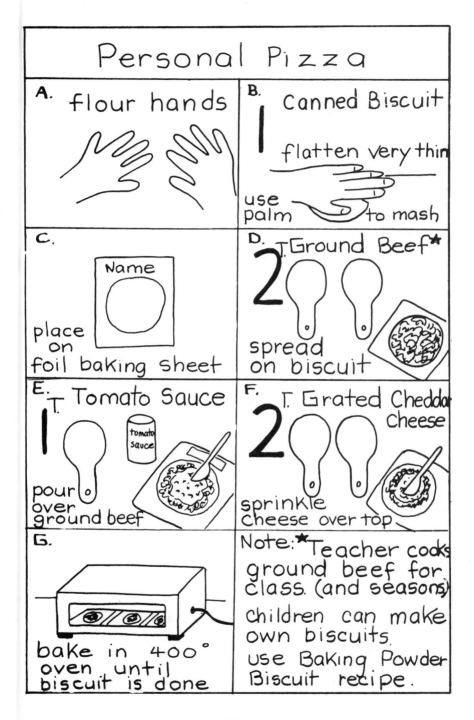

A. flour hands

B. Canned Biscuit

flatten very thin

use palm to mash

C. Name

place on foil baking sheet

D. 2 T. Ground Beef★

spread on biscuit

E. 1 T. Tomato Sauce

tomato sauce

pour over ground beef

F. 2 T. Grated Cheddar cheese

sprinkle cheese over top

G. bake in 400° oven until biscuit is done

Note: ★Teacher cooks ground beef for class. (and seasons)

children can make own biscuits.

use Baking Powder Biscuit recipe.

Tasting Time

Objective: To taste all foods served at school or Day Care center

Materials:

* Blindfold (optional)
* 1 teaspoon for each child
* ½ -¾ cup of each food to be tasted.
* 1 serving teaspoon for each food to be tasted in room.

Procedure: During quiet time in the room, preceeding lunch time, children take turns going to the tasting tray.

Teacher serves a taste into each childs spoon. Children may be blindfolded to guess what they are tasting.

Two Kindergarten classes began this game the first day of school-1977. Continued daily through November.

Results: much better acceptance of cafeteria food than found in previous classes.

Information Relative To U.S.D.A. Food Pattern Guidelines

⬤ The following, made with enriched flour meet the standards for supplemental foods:

⬤ The following could be included as part of the supplemental food pattern or lunch:

Abbreviations used in recipes:

t.   teaspoon
T.   tablespoon
ml.   milliliter
cm.   centimeter

Equivalent Weights and Measures

1 pinch . . . . as much as can be pinched between the tip of the finger and the thumb
60 drops . . . . 1 teaspoon
3 teaspoons . . . . 1 tablespoon
4 tablespoons . . . . ¼ cup
5⅓ tablespoons . . . . ⅓ cup
8 tablespoons . . . . ½ cup
16 tablespoons . . . . 1 cup
margarine ¼ lb. . . . . 8 tablespoons (½ cup)
granulated sugar (1 lb.) . . . . 2¼ cups
brown sugar (1 lb.) . . . . 2 cups packed
1 medium egg . . . . 4 tablespoons (for easier measuring add 1 teaspoon water to egg and mix well)
Apples (1 lb.) . . . . 3 medium (3 cups diced)
Cheese, American ¼ lb. . . . . 16 tablespoons (grated)
Cheese, cottage ½ pint. . . . . 16 tablespoons
Cheese, cream ½ pint . . . . 16 tablespoons
Lemon, 1 medium . . . . 3 tablespoons juice
Gingerbread mix (14.5 oz. box) . makes 16 to 18 individual portion recipes, depending on spillage and waste

Metric Conversion

Metric measuring spoons may be used instead of traditional measuring spoons.

Measuring spoons and cups are available marked with traditional as well as metric measurements as follows:

1 t.	=	5 ml.	1 cup	=	240 ml.
1/8 t.	=	.6 ml.	1/4 cup	=	60 ml.
1/4 t.	=	1.2 ml.	1/3 cup	=	80 ml.
1/2 t.	=	2.5 ml.	1/2 cup	=	120 ml.
1 T.	=	15 ml.	3/4 cup	=	180 ml.
1/2 T.	=	7.5 ml.	2/3 cup	=	160 ml.